DEATH VALLEY

NATURAL WONDERS

Jason Cooper

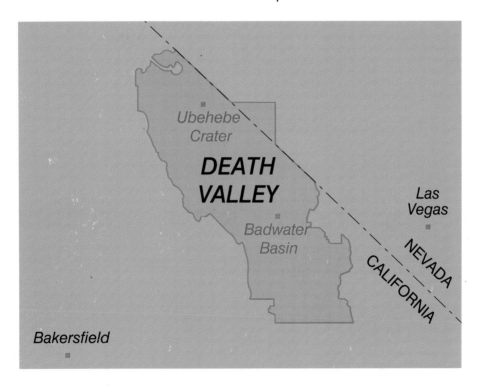

The Rourke Press, Inc.
Vero Beach, Florida 32964

PHOTO CREDITS
Cover, p. 17, © Jerry Hennen; p. 4, 10, 12, 15 © Robin and Craig
Brandt; p. 7 © Joel Gallin; p. 8, 13, 18, 21 © Steve Warble

Library of Congress Cataloging-in-Publication Data

Cooper, Jason, 1942-
   Death Valley / Jason Cooper
      p. cm. — (Natural Wonders)
   Includes index.
   ISBN 1-57103-015-8
   1. Death Valley (Calif. and Nev.)—Juvenile literature.
2. Death Valley National Monument (Calif. and Nev.)—Juvenile liter-
ature.
[1. Death Valley (Calif. and Nev.) 2. Death Valley National
Monument (Calif. and Nev.) 3. National parks and reserves.]
I. Title II. Series
F868.D2C66 1995
979.4' 87—dc20
                                     95–12306
                                        CIP
                                        AC

Printed in the USA

TABLE OF CONTENTS

DEATH VALLEY

If Alaska is America's icebox, Death Valley is its fireplace. The second hottest temperature ever recorded anywhere—134 degrees Fahrenheit—was in Death Valley.

Death Valley is a great trench flanked by mountain slopes. It is about 130 miles long and six to 14 miles across. Most of it lies in east central California. A small portion extends into Nevada.

Winters are mild, but fiery summer heat bakes Death Valley, making foot travel risky

THE MOJAVE DESERT

Death Valley is part of the **Mojave Desert** (mo HAH vee DEZ ert). Like all deserts, the Mojave is quite dry. Most of Death Valley receives less than two inches of rain each year.

Most of the Mojave is high, **shrubby** (SHRUH bee) ground, between 2,000 and 5,000 feet above sea level. Death Valley, however, lies below sea level. In fact, Death Valley is the lowest dry land in the western half of the world!

California's Mojave is mostly shrubby, upland desert

PLANTS

Despite Death Valley's summer heat, over 600 **species** (SPEE sheez), or kinds, of plants grow there. Some of them are cactuses, like the prickly cholla.

Among the most common large plants are creosote bushes, burro bushes, and mesquite trees. Death Valley also has groves of unusual Joshua trees, sometimes called tree yuccas. These tall, spindly plants have long, dagger-like leaves.

Death Valley sun sets behind a prickly screen of cholla cactus thorns

ANIMALS

Hot desert country is ideal for many kinds of animals. Fifty-three kinds of mammals live in Death Valley. Thirty-six kinds of reptiles—snakes, lizards and turtles—live there. Death Valley has 230 kinds of birds and several species of rare, minnow-sized pupfish. Pupfish live in the valley's streams, springs, and salty marshes.

Bobcats, coyotes, and kit foxes visit Death Valley to hunt mice, rabbits, and birds. Death Valley's biggest plant eaters are desert bighorn sheep.

A coyote pauses from its rabbit hunt in Death Valley

Death Valley dunes rise in waves of sand

Ubehebe Crater was carved several thousand years ago by a steam explosion under the surface of Death Valley

PEOPLE IN DEATH VALLEY

In 1849 a small band of pioneers wandered into the Mojave Desert wilderness. They found themselves struggling in a long, deep valley. After two months they escaped with their lives, but with little else. They called the valley that had nearly killed them Death Valley.

In later years, prospectors hunted for gold and silver in Death Valley. The valley had little of either, but it was rich in another mineral—**borax** (BOR ax).

Hikers climb a sand dune in Death Valley during the coolness of spring

BORAX

Borax is one of many valuable materials found in the ground. It is used in household cleaners, fuels, fertilizers, drugs, paints, nonstick coatings and other products.

In the 1870's, a mining company shipped borax from Death Valley in wagons drawn by teams of 20 mules. The mule "trains" took 10 days to reach the railroad, 165 miles away.

Borax is still mined in the California desert, but not in Death Valley.

Block walls and wooden wagons once drawn by mules are reminders of Death Valley's Harmony Borax Works

DEATH VALLEY NATIONAL PARK

Because of its natural beauty, much of Death Valley was set aside in 1933 for public use. Death Valley became a fully protected national park in 1994. With over 3,000,000 acres, it also became America's largest national park outside Alaska.

Death Valley National Park includes more than the desert valley. It has mountain wilderness, springs, waterfalls, and many **historic** (hiss TOR ihk) places.

Dawn brightens the wind-and-water worn rocks of Zabriskie Point in Death Valley National Park

19

SEASONS

A "cool" summer day in Death Valley may be 110 degrees Fahrenheit. The ground temperature at Badwater in the valley can reach 200 degrees. The heat rises through shoes!

Late fall, winter, and early spring are more comfortable. Daytime temperatures are often in the 60's and 70's. Light snow powders mountain heights in winter.

In spring, the valley may erupt in a colorful riot of wildflowers.

Hikers approach the salty pools at Badwater, reflecting the Panamint Mountains

WONDERS OF DEATH VALLEY

Deserts are not dull. The Death Valley area is full of wonderfully weird rocks, craters, sand dunes, salty plains, and colorful hills. Desert plants and animals abound.

The Devil's Golf Course is a "garden" of strange rocks. At the open place called the Race Track, winds push rocks like marbles across the sand.

At Badwater, visitors stand on one of the lowest spots on Earth, 282 feet below sea level. Yet, within hiking distance, Telescope Peak rears up—11,000 feet above sea level.

Glossary

borax (BOR ax) — a white mineral mined from the California desert and used for cleaning powders and other products

historic (hiss TOR ihk) — of some importance in the history of a place

Mojave Desert (mo HAH vee DEZ ert) — the particular desert of southeastern California and southern Nevada

shrubby (SHRUH bee) — referring to an area of shrubs—plants with several stems and about four to 12 feet tall

species (SPEE sheez) — a certain kind of animal within a closely related group; for example, a *kit* fox

INDEX